The S Word Workbook

A Sales Book for Business Owners

by Rob Bedell

ISBN: 978-1707917204

First Edition: November, 2019

Book cover design: Dana Paris
Editing: Kirsten Rees | MakeMeASuccess

This is a companion workbook to *The S Word* book which I recommend you purchase before using this workbook. This can be used alongside the book or afterwards to take action.

For information contact:
LinkedIn: https://www.linkedin.com/in/robbedell/

Table of Contents

Thank you for reading The S Word and learning more about sales; the lifeblood of your business. On first read, there should be at least a few takeaways which you can take action in your own business/life and then this workbook will help you take that even further. We'll recap those important topics, as well as let you work through the other areas which will help you build a more solid sales model for your business.

First, let's recap some of the foundation of sales to ensure it sinks in. Sales is simply _____. If you get this and your sales team gets this, it will help them from getting stuck in their heads and when they do, it helps you get them unstuck. Is there more to sales than that? Yes, but this is the foundation and even without techniques or methods to use, it will help bring in more on the lower level sales.

Sales is like the human body, two _____, one _____. If you're not asking questions, you'll never know their needs. It's great when your sales team knows everything about what you have to offer but what good is it if they don't know how that benefits others. Ask your question then SHUT UP! Listen! When you listen, do you hear problems you can help with? Did you hear something which causes them pain? What can you save them? Time? Money? Effort?

Before you start that conversation, a few things should happen. First, what is your value proposition? Do you remember? If not, let's build it out so you and your whole company know it. Your whole company repeats it. Your whole company lets it become a roar, every time they talk about your company!

Remember, this is not what you think your value is. It is what your clients are saying. "Well Rob, we're a start-up and don't have clients/customers yet. What do we do?" I'm glad you asked. It should be included in your market surveys. You are having a test market, a beta product/service that people can test, right? What are they saying? This will change as your business grows.

Even if you have clients and have asked them, go out to new clients once a year and ask them the question again, why do you work with us? Ask it every year to new clients and to some of the same clients. The answers may change and when they do, you want to be on top of it. Use that feedback to create and recreate your value proposition.

Why do people like working with you? What problems do you solve? What do you make easier? What do you not miss, that other companies do? It doesn't have to be long and it shouldn't be. It's your elevator pitch. You should be able to cover it in 20-30 seconds. Write it down:

CHAPTER 1

Value Proposition

Write down your value proposition here.

_____
_____
_____
_____
_____
_____
_____
_____

Now you have your value proposition. Have everyone write it out. Print it out and post it in various places throughout your office. Put it on your website. Put it on your printed materials. Make sure your sales team knows it. Make sure your management knows it. Make sure your accounting, your marketing, your warehouse, your production, your every department and every single person knows it.

When a couple of salespeople know it, their voices can get drowned out. But when your whole company says it, chants it, take it to heart, it becomes a roar. Make your company ROAR!

CHAPTER 2

Competition

Do you know your competition? Who else is in your industry, in your space? What do you do better? What do they do better? (BE HONEST!!!)

Company: Pros: Cons:
1._____   _____   _____
2._____   _____   _____
3._____   _____   _____
4._____   _____   _____
5._____   _____   _____

In most industries, you will only have a couple of main companies to compete with but you can list up to five here. If there are more than five, then most likely, there is not a leader in the industry, which gives you a great opportunity to establish yourself as one.

What are the three things which make you stand out? (It doesn't need to be three but it's a good number to shoot for.) What do you do better? Faster? More completely? What three things would make me want to work with you and your company?

1._____
_____
_____
_____
_____

2._____
_____
_____
_____
_____

3._____
_____
_____
_____
_____

Hopefully one of those things is customer service. If not applicable, then maybe a money-back guarantee. Something that will make them feel more comfortable giving you their money. What can you do or say that will make someone reach for their wallet, cut that check, give you their credit card and feel at ease doing it? If you were your customer/client, what would you want?

This point should always be the last point. "Yes, our {insert product/service} has the highest quality in the industry, that means you get more from it for longer. This makes doing your job easier and without fear of it breaking down every other month. And if you ever do have a problem, all you do is contact us and we'll overnight a replacement to you. No worries at all!"

Best quality in the industry

Makes your job easier without pause.

Replacement overnight, if any issue arises.

You can make your reasons a simple or complex as you want, but remember, the simpler it is, the easier it is for people to do business with you. Plus, say something different than what everyone else in your space is saying.

Remember, at the insurance inspection company mentioned in the book, everyone was saying quality and time service. We changed it to customer service and communication and it made us stand out. What will make you stand out and not blend into the dull buzz everyone else is saying? Stand out!!

CHAPTER 3

Your Ideal Client

As I mentioned in the book, not everyone is your client, your customer. Plus, you don't want everyone as your customer. Seriously, do you want that one client that takes up all of your time, is really frustrating, and you don't add much on the bottom line when you work with them? NO!!! If you focus on the ideal client, the ideal customer adding the most to your bottom line and not taking up unneeded resources, i.e time and effort, you will be more profitable and your staff will be happier.

First, you must find your ideal client. Who are they? Where are they? Once you define these, you'll be able to find them easier.

Who are they? If customers (people), what demographic make-up are they? Age? Income? Sex? What's their lifestyle? If they are clients (businesses), what are their demographic make-up? What size company? What revenue? What industries? What level in the business do they live? C-level? Owner/manager?

Now, this is some of the high-level key identifiers. You can drill down, and you will as you get more experience. But this gives you a place to start.

Where are they? Where do they go physically, what do they read? Where do they go online? Do they go to forums? Are there industry-specific websites they visit?

Why is this so important? When I started my consulting business, I didn't have this defined. I was trying to help everyone. I could help a lot of businesses in a lot of different areas, so I felt it was the best thing to do. It wasn't until the President of my local Chamber of Commerce sat me down and said this when it finally made sense. "Rob, you're a smart guy. You seem to know a lot and work with a lot of different companies in a lot of different areas. But what is it that you do?"

What did I do? Who was my ideal client? The next week, I sat down and defined this. It started rather broad, which I recommend. But as I started to go through it more and more, it was clear that I helped small businesses get more money for their businesses. As soon as I defined this, I found all of the businesses who needed my help. It was easier to find them because I knew who I was looking for and could see them when I spoke to them.

Will it come that easy for every business, maybe not. But if you don't know who you are looking for, you will never find them. So, define your ideal client. Make copies of the next page. Your ideal client may change, as your business grows.

CHAPTER 4

Ideal Customer

Again, this starts really broad. You will find other more specific identifiers are you drill down more but this will give you a place to start from.

_____	_____	_____	_____
Age	Sex	Income Level	Area/location

Hobbies/lifestyle

_____	_____	_____	_____
Home Owner/Renter	Education Level	Occupation	Ethnicity

Clients:

_____	_____	_____
Industry	Company Size	Annual Revenue

_____	_____
Decision Maker Title	Location

CHAPTER 5

Lead Scoring

Now we know bad leads are EVIL and can kill your sales and sales team. We want to score every lead that comes in so we can find the good lead sources and which ones we need to stop getting. It would be great if you could find a lead source with all pre-qualified leads and you may, at a tradeshow or event where you have a strong presence. But if you are getting leads from any other source, you will most likely have to score them to see how good they are.

I am going to give a very high-level scoring system you can start with. You may have more levels as you build out your sales process, but this will help you get started.

Do they need your product/service? Yes - 20% No - 0% dead lead

Is the contact information correct? Yes - 20% No - 0% dead lead

Can you get them on the phone? Yes - 20%, No - 0%

Did you give a proposal? Yes - 20%, No - 0%.

Did they accept? Yes - 20%, No - 0%.

If your leads from a particular source do not clear 40%, stop getting those leads! If your leads get stuck between 40-80%, you may need to adjust your sales process or provide more training to have better conversations and create better proposals. These may not be bad leads. You may just need to work on things internally. Once you get those areas corrected, if little to none get to 80-100%, then you might want a different lead source. If all of your leads get to 80-100%, then that is a good lead source. If you are not having enough get to 100%, try working on your proposal or your main offering.

Regardless, when you put in lead scoring, you will get a better idea of good lead sources, where you need training and how good your proposal or offerings are. You can adjust your lead source, your training, your proposals, or what you may need to change in what you are offering. You will have more information from which to make business decisions.

CHAPTER 6

Your Sales Process

You may know the question I ask every business owner I work with, "If I came to work at your business, in a sales capacity, and wanted to blow the doors off of sales, what do I have to do?" This is where I get a lot of blank stares. And it's understandable.

Most business owners don't know sales. That's not their background. They figure they can just hire someone to do that. But what happens when sales are down, or they feel they should be getting more sales? They ask the person running sales and get this answer or that answer. They don't really know if the answers are real or just excuses. It's because of that confusion that I think every business owner, or person running a business, needs to understand the sales process. How do you figure out what that is? One stage at a time.

The sales process will vary from business to business, industry to industry, type of client to type of client. So it's hard to give you a model which will work for every business but I can give you an outline to work from. You can fill in the details.

Stage one: leads and first contact. This is where you take your lead and qualify them. Do they need what you have and is the contact information correct? Yes? They get passed stage one. No? They get discarded.

Stage two: first contact. This is where you have your talking points and questions ready. What questions are you asking? What did they say in response? You may have a marketing one-sheet to send out at the end of the call. This is where you figure out what needs to be covered in the first contact, who needs to be involved and what materials need to be given out. Is a presentation needed? Can everything be covered without one? Did you cover all of your talking points and get answers to all of your questions? Yes, go to the next stage. No, go back and get what you need before moving forward.

Stage three: questions/objections. This is where you answer any questions they may have and cover any objections that come up. Are they using a competitor? What do you do better? What do they need to make their decision? Did you cover all of their questions and have ways to overcome their objections to their content? Yes, go to stage four. No, go back and answer them or find answers for them before moving on.

Stage four: the proposal. What do you recommend and why? AND WHY?!?! I see so many salespeople do presentations showing what they will be getting and even how it will benefit them. The benefit should tell them why, right? No. The WHY comes from what they've said in response to the questions. It is critically important to use the WHY. It closes more sales! When you say, "Hey Doug, remember when you said you had that problem? You see how this will help? And Susie, remember you said you had a hard time with this? See how much easier this will make it?" It reminds them why they need to buy from your team! Did you close the sale? Yes, give them a contract or set them up. No? Where did you lose them? Document it. See if it's a regular occurrence and if so, get training involved.

Stage five: advocacy. Yes, after you get the sale, you still have work to do. You do the work to keep the sale. What training does the new client need? What is going to be delivered and when? Walk them through the timeline and make sure they understand it. Make sure you have your point of contact and they have yours. How often should you contact them? What needs to happen for you to contact them? You'd be surprised at how many sales are lost because this stage is not done.

Once a quarter, ask questions and inform. Are they happy? Are you doing a good job? What else can you help them with? What has changed on your side? What's changed on their side?

As I said, you may have more stages or you may have less. If you only have two or three stages, you are probably missing something. If you have over six or seven, you may have some stages in that you don't need. Doing a presentation is NOT a stage! It may be part of a stage, but your goal should not be to do a presentation. Your goal should be to make the sale. If you need to do a presentation, do one. If you don't. DON'T!!

Here are some rules of thumb. Does this stage advance the prospect in their buying process? Does your sales stage match one of their buying stages? What needs to happen in order for you to know you have gone passed this stage? What materials do you need to share? Who needs to be involved on your side and on their side?

Now it's time to write out your stages and what is involved in each. **** When you first do this, don't get too caught up in your head. Write down what you think. You can always go back and edit as you move forward. As a matter of FACT, this will change as your company grows, as the market changes, as what you offer changes. Just start! ****

Again, here is a basic sales process you can work from. You can adjust it, tweak it, completely change it depending on your business, industry, company, etc. But it gives you something to work from:

Qualify - Do they need what you have? Can you give them what they need? Are they ready to incorporate what you have? This means, if what you have would add 30% new business to them, can they process that business. Are you ready to handle their business? Same thing in reverse.

Educate - This goes two ways. Starting with your education. What are their main needs? What problems they have that you can solve? Can you show them how you can help them? Will this be mutually beneficial?

Propose - Do you both agree on what is needed on both sides for this to be successful. Get a verbal agreement you see it is mutually beneficial. Many people skip this step and it comes back to bite them when they start working together. The client may not fully understand what is needed on their side. Time to learn. Time to train. People that are needed on their side. People needed on your side.

Contract - This goes into the details about the new relationship. What each side will give and what each side will get.

Advocacy - What needs to happen after the sale? Who needs to be involved and introduced to the new arrangement. Regular follow up to ensure it is working. This is another step a lot of businesses forget which can result in losing clients.

You can make copies of the next page, one page per stage. As you edit and update each stage, replace it but I always recommend keeping what you had before. You never know when you should go back to what you used to do.

Stage ___: _____

               Name of stage

What is your main goal of this stage?

_____

_____

_____

What points/materials need to be covered?

_____

_____

_____

_____

Who needs to be involved?
On your side?

_____

_____

On their side?

_____

_____

What needs to happen to know you have completed this stage?

_____

_____

_____

_____

CHAPTER 7

What Does Your Company Look Like?
How Do You Want to be Represented?

The first part of this is how does your company sound? Are they a bunch of voices lost in the wind, or are they in unison creating a roar? This goes back to your value proposition. Pull that out again. Walk around and see if everyone knows it. Do this regularly. It may seem like too much but it's not. Once it becomes muscle memory for everyone at the company, then you can back off a little. Once everyone has it, it becomes a little bit of goofy fun.

If after reading the book I say to you, "When common sense becomes common practice, ...? You can probably finish that for me. You may roll your eyes but you'll also smile and get it. Create that in your company.

Now that everyone sounds the same, how do you want them to look? How do you want your company to be represented? In today's business world, the idea of walking around in a three-piece suit is probably not what you want. Or maybe it is, that's up to you.

Do you have uniforms? Do you have the same shirt you want people to wear? Do you want them to be casual because they all work inside on the phones? Do you want them to be business casual?

Again, one thing you can do to help you decide is to take a look at your customers. Dress one level above them. Take a look at your competition. Do you want to look like them? Are they too stiff? Are they too casual? There is no one right answer for everyone. You need to do what works for you and your company but don't NOT make a decision. Think about it! Come to a conclusion and maybe an agreement within your company. This is one that can be a group decision, but ultimately, it falls to you to make the final decision.

Here are some questions to help:
Our customers see our team regularly? _____
Our clients' dress code is _____
Our competition's dress code is _____
When clients/prospects see our staff, we want them to think _____
What type of salespeople do you have? _____
What motivates each one? _____

CHAPTER 8

Treat Everyone Fairly, But Not the Same!!

I hope you fully understand that statement. If you have kids, you probably get it. Notice I said kids with an S. I don't have kids but I have nieces and a nephew. I see how each are very different. They all respond to different motivation factors. They all push for different incentives. One likes money. One likes recognition. Another does things because it just needs to get done. That being the case, I treat them all fairly but not the same.

It's the same with salespeople. The biggest mistake most business owners make is thinking all salespeople are only motivated by money. That is NOT the case and actually, most really good salespeople, are motivated by other factors.

This is not to say money is a non-factor, especially at the beginning of a salesperson's sales career. I remember first starting in sales. My first year, I earned a little over $14,000, but that was for only half a year. My next year, I doubled that easily. Then it kept going up. I remember every year when I earned more than I ever earned before. I kept pushing, but as I got closer to six figures and clearing it, while it was still a factor, it wasn't the biggest factor.

I knew I could make more money. I knew that if I went to a different company or a different industry, I could make well into six figures. However, I enjoyed being part of a company's growth and future, more than anything. I liked the recognition.

So, what motivates your salespeople? What motivates your sales team? You should know what motivates them individually and as a team. Most likely, they are two different things. Use the following worksheet for each person on your sales team. Make sure your sales leader has access to this as well, so they know how to coach them.

_____
Salesperson Name

_____
How much money do you want to make?

_____
What are your thoughts on a work/life balance?

_____
What hobbies do you have?

_____
Where do you like to go on vacation?

_____
Which would you rather have, an upgrade to your car or a week vacation to your favorite place?

_____
Would you rather be really rich and live a secluded life, or well-to-do and famous?

_____
Which appeals to you more, a free dinner and show on the town or a $500 bonus?

_____
What do you want to get out of your career in the next five years?

_____
Where do you want to grow the most personally in the next five years?

CHAPTER 9

How to Coach Your Team and Coaching Drills

Treat everyone on your sales team fairly but not the same!! Yes, it's worth repeating.

Now, you have your salespeople's profiles. You know if they are motivated by money or attention or something else. This will show you how to coach each person. Do they want public attention or recognized in private? Do they want more time off with their family and friends, or more money? Are they looking to move forward in their career, or just do their job and have a life outside of work?

All of these points will show you how to coach and motivate each person. An important part to this is when having one on one meetings with people who don't like public attention, you let them know why you celebrate their successes in closed-door meetings. You do this just in case, down the line, they decide that it's ok to talk about it at meetings or on the sales floor.

Coaching is selling at a different level and it is also like the human body with two ears, one mouth. Once you give guidance, encouragement or praise, stop talking and listen. How did they respond to what you just said. Was it positive? Were they unresponsive? Did they roll their eyes?

If it was positive, great, you are coaching them the way they want. They are giving you the reaction you wanted and expected. Continue coaching them in the same manner, but always pay attention to see if it changes at any points.

If there are indifferent, why? Are they having a bad day? Is their mind somewhere else? Do they just not care? It could be a combination of things. How do you know? How do you figure it out? Ask!

How's it going today? Is everything alright? You seem distracted today, can I help with anything? Sometimes people aren't even aware when they are not present. If something is on their mind, they may not see the way they are acting, so sometimes, you need to pull it out of them. That's what coaches do.

Coaches also figure out when a person on their team is not motivated. When they are not taking what they are doing seriously. They roll their eyes. They sigh a lot. They breathe heavier. Sometimes, this is when the coach needs to be direct and ask what is happening. "What's up?" Are they happy? Do they not want to be there? You can give them the training and tools to be successful but not the will to want to be there. They need to be honest with you and themselves. You'd be surprised at what a little honesty can do.

CHAPTER 10

Metrics - What are You Watching? Why?

As I said before, I don't look at the number of calls made. I don't look at how many presentations were done or how long they were. The only metric I look at is what I want, sales! How many sales were brought in during the sales period? But this can change a little depending on the sales role. Here are some questions to ask to determine how you measure the sales numbers:

Do you have salespeople that only get paid on new sales and someone else, i.e. account manager, maintains the accounts?

Do your salespeople sell and maintain the accounts?

What is your sales cycle? If short, how many do you expect to be closed in a sales period? If longer, does it take time to build up to closing?

What is your industry standard? I.e. what is everyone else doing? This doesn't mean you want to be closing the same as everyone else but it gives something to measure against.

Having these metrics will help you in setting goals for your salespeople and your sales team. It can, and most likely will, change as your business grows, market conditions change, or what you have changes. But again, you need a starting point, so this will help you get started.

CHAPTER 11

Who is Responsible for What?

A big problem with small businesses is clarity on who is responsible for what. In big corporations, every position has a job description with responsibilities attached to each. Some small businesses do have job descriptions, but they don't always include what they are responsible for fully. They may have broad, sweeping statements without specifics.

The sales manager is responsible for all sales activities and making sure the department reaches its goals. What does that mean? Do they just yell at the sales team to get them to sell? Or do they coach and support them with training tools?

They need to write up monthly reports on the progress of the sales team and each of its members. What needs to be included in this report? It is what the sales leader thinks of each person, or strictly based on numbers? What do you, the person who runs the business, want to know? Do you want to just know the numbers? Do you want a breakdown of each salesperson? Do you just want a couple of paragraphs summarizing what happened during the last sales period and plans for what they will do during the next one?

You have to decide what you want to see but you may want a mix of numbers and assessment. What number did the department get to, how and why? What number did each salesperson get to, how and why? You can keep it that simple or break down into more specifics. Who were the biggest clients in regards to revenue this period? Who were the new clients brought in this period and who landed them? Who did we lose? Why?

You also can change what you need in your report depending on the success or lack thereof. You can start with the more general summary and if the numbers aren't where they need to be, then you can ask for more specifics. I was used to giving a general summary and then answering the specifics when asked. This way, I gave them what they needed without having them burdened with a long, lengthy report. But when they needed to the details, I had them.

The following page will show you examples of both. What you will want is up to you, but I don't know if you need all of the details, unless you see issues starting to surface, i.e. the numbers are falling or not growing.

Department Summary

Department Name:_____

Period Goal: _____

Period Number: _____

New Clients This Period:_____

Number of Clients Lost:_____

Summary:

Department Breakdown:

Department Name:_____

Period Goal: _____

Period Number: _____

New Clients This Period:_____

Name of new clients and salesperson associated:

Number of Clients Lost:_____

Name of new clients and salesperson associated:

Salesperson Name:_____

Goal:_____   Number:_____

New Accounts:_____

Accounts Lost:_____

Summary:

(Repeat per rep)

CHAPTER 12

How to Run a Sales Meeting

Sales meetings can be a complete waste of time if they are not run properly. As I stated in the book, sales meetings are not the place to cover policies and procedures. Can you introduce new products? Yes. That impacts sales. Can you cover the new systems to enter orders? No. That should be a memo and short meeting to answer questions. Team sales meetings are to cover sales. Did you meet the goal? What were the successes? What areas do we need to focus on? What tools are being used?

You noticed I said team sales meetings. In individual sales meetings, you can cover accounts that were lost and why. You can cover individual successes if they don't like public attention. At team sales meetings, you cover account successes, if the salesperson doesn't want personal attention. This is where you get your team excited about what they do. This is where you give them all of the tools to be successful. This is where you repeat the value proposition and have everyone repeat it to show they are all on the same page and understand why what you offer is so great. This is the meeting you want everyone walking out of excited and ready to talk to prospects and turn them into clients.

How do you do this? Keep it strictly to sales and don't get distracted. Offer times for other meetings to cover topics that are not going to bring in new sales during the next sales period. Here are some points to follow:

Goal for period.

Number for period. (Congratulate success, what more we can offer to reach it next time. Go through metrics if needed be but stay focused on sales)

Talk about new clients and how they were landed.

Talk about new offers.

Sales tip.

Goal for next period. Let's go get it!! Mention any bonus for hitting goal.

If any topics come up which don't directly affect sales for this or next period, say, "If you want, we can set up a different time to cover that. Talk to me after this meeting to schedule it." If they feel it's important, they'll set it up. If there were just trying to be distracting, they won't. Stay positive. Stay upbeat. Stay motivating!!

REVIEW YEARLY

You should do a yearly review, if not quarterly - put your next review in your calendar now. These questions can be used for either:

What has changed at your company?
What has changed in what you offer?
What has changed in the market?
Who are new players in the industry?
Who are the white whale clients?
What technology changes have happened?

Use this workbook regularly. Use it to set up your sales, sales team and sales process. Use it for on-going coaching for the team, managing for the numbers, and process. Change your plan when needed and when it's not working. When you have your process in place, you should be able to see where sales are getting stuck and figure out if it's the process or more training is needed.

When you and your team use this workbook, you will understand sales much more and it won't be the scary, unknown part of your business. Now you will understand your sales and be able to help grow it.

Connect with me on:
LinkedIn: https://www.linkedin.com/in/robbedell/
Website: Robbedell.com